4-6

Fisher
  True-life monsters of the
prehistoric skies

TRUE-LIFE MONSTERS OF THE PREHISTORIC SKIES

For a free color catalog describing Gareth Stevens' list of high-quality books and multimedia programs, call 1-800-542-2595 (USA) or 1-800-461-9120 (Canada). Gareth Stevens Publishing's Fax: (414) 225-0377.

Library of Congress Cataloging-in-Publication Data

Fisher, Enid.
    True-life monsters of the prehistoric skies/by Enid Fisher;
illustrated by Richard Grant.
      p. cm. — (World of dinosaurs)
    Includes bibliographical references and index.
    Summary: Examines the different kinds of prehistoric flying
reptiles known as pterosaurs, who ruled the skies while the dinosaurs
ruled the earth, discussing their flight, nesting and feeding habits,
and relationship to birds.
    ISBN 0-8368-2294-3 (lib. bdg.)
    1. Pterosauria—Juvenile literature. [1. Pterosaurs.] I. Grant, Richard,
1959- ill. II. Title. III. Series: World of dinosaurs.
QE862.P7F57   1999
567.918—dc21   98-45732

This North American edition first published in 1999 by
Gareth Stevens Publishing
1555 North RiverCenter Drive, Suite 201
Milwaukee, Wisconsin 53212 USA

This U.S. edition © 1999 by Gareth Stevens, Inc.
Created with original © 1998 by Quartz Editorial Services,
112 Station Road, Edgware HA8 7AQ U.K.
Additional end matter © 1999 by Gareth Stevens, Inc.

Consultant: Dr. Paul Barrett, Paleontologist, Specialist in Biology and
  Evolution of Dinosaurs, University of Cambridge, England.

Printed in Mexico

1 2 3 4 5 6 7 8 9 03 02 01 00 99

TRUE-LIFE MONSTERS OF THE PREHISTORIC SKIES

by Enid Fisher
Illustrated by Richard Grant

Gareth Stevens Publishing
MILWAUKEE

CONTENTS

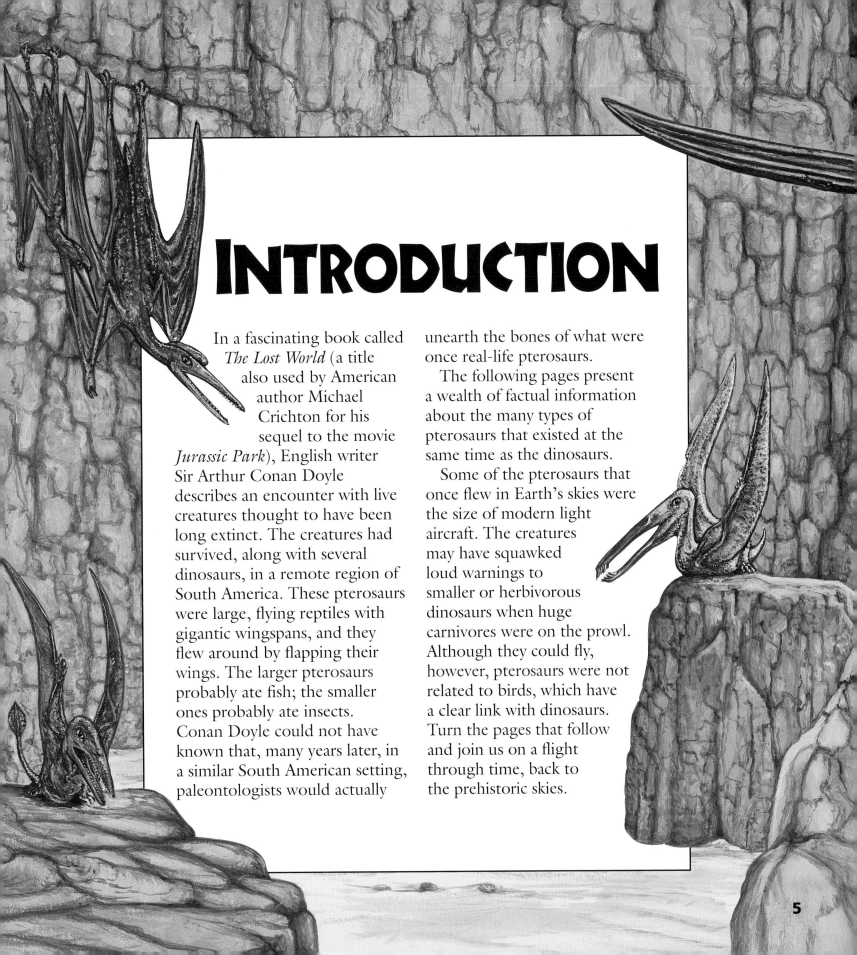

INTRODUCTION

In a fascinating book called *The Lost World* (a title also used by American author Michael Crichton for his sequel to the movie *Jurassic Park*), English writer Sir Arthur Conan Doyle describes an encounter with live creatures thought to have been long extinct. The creatures had survived, along with several dinosaurs, in a remote region of South America. These pterosaurs were large, flying reptiles with gigantic wingspans, and they flew around by flapping their wings. The larger pterosaurs probably ate fish; the smaller ones probably ate insects. Conan Doyle could not have known that, many years later, in a similar South American setting, paleontologists would actually unearth the bones of what were once real-life pterosaurs.

The following pages present a wealth of factual information about the many types of pterosaurs that existed at the same time as the dinosaurs.

Some of the pterosaurs that once flew in Earth's skies were the size of modern light aircraft. The creatures may have squawked loud warnings to smaller or herbivorous dinosaurs when huge carnivores were on the prowl. Although they could fly, however, pterosaurs were not related to birds, which have a clear link with dinosaurs. Turn the pages that follow and join us on a flight through time, back to the prehistoric skies.

THE DRAGON CONNECTION

Some scientists have suggested that the dragons of ancient myth may not just be the product of storytellers' active imaginations, but a primitive attempt at explaining pterosaur fossils.

As the sky started to darken, everyone instinctively knew that the dreaded dragon was coming. Terrified, the people hid in caves as its monstrous, scaly, bright orange body, carried by huge, leathery wings, swooped down from the heavens and threatened to devour any creature that stood in its way. Fierce flames shot forth from its gaping mouth and soon reduced the hillsides of waving corn to blackened stubble. At last, it zoomed away, and everyone slowly crept out from their hiding places, glad, at least, that they had escaped the dragon's attack.

The folklore of many countries includes tales of dragons. The English story of St. George, for example, tells how he killed just such a creature. Other stories tell of dragons that inhabited caves, guarding treasure. All accounts, however, refer to them as looking like lizards, with scaly skin, four clawed feet, and jointed, flapping wings. Not all of the monsters breathed fire, but most regularly devoured crops or people.

Ancient explanations

Some experts believe that the dragons of Chinese legend may have developed from the accidental discovery of dinosaur fossils long before anyone recognized them for what they were. Not all Chinese depictions of dragons had wings, so it is possible that some dragon stories were a way of making sense of any huge dinosaur bones that were found embedded in prehistoric rocks. In fact, the Chinese word for dragon — *kung-lung* — is exactly the same as the word they use for a dinosaur.

Pterosaur look-alikes

The dragons described in Western literature dating from medieval times right up to the seventeenth century also bear a resemblance to what experts think pterosaurs must have looked like, judging from their fossils. Many of these legends originated in northern Europe, where several important pterosaur finds have been made. For example, the tale of a treasure-guarding dragon named Fafnir is immortalized by the nineteenth-century German composer Wagner in his opera *Siegfried*. This may, of course, be a coincidence; but, if so, it is a remarkable one.

THE FIRST PTEROSAUR FIND

The very first pterosaur fossils were found in Germany in the late eighteenth century. It was many years later, however, before the experts of that time were able to decide what kind of creature it must have been.

As it munched a meal of damp leaves, the Triassic herbivore **Sellosaurus** suddenly felt something land on its back and wondered what was happening. Curious, it turned its long, snakelike neck and saw that a few pterosaurs had chosen to use its bulky body as a landing strip.

The first realization that flying creatures unlike any other animals alive today may have existed in the prehistoric past came when a jumble of fossilized bones was examined by the eighteenth-century Italian naturalist Cosimo Collini. Collini was in charge of a natural history collection housed in the palace of the Elector Karl Theodor, in Mannheim, in southern Germany.

The bones had been unearthed in local limestone quarries at Eichstätt sometime between 1767 and 1784. At first, Collini thought they may have come from a sea creature, but he could not explain the legs. He also felt sure that a membrane must have been attached to the extraordinarily long arm bones of this creature, enabling it to fly, but he was also convinced it was not a bird.

Named at last

When the French anatomy expert Georges Cuvier came across an engraving of the find in 1801, he immediately recognized the bones as those of a reptile. He, too, was convinced that the creature had been able to fly, and so he named it *Ptero-dactyle*, or "flight-finger." Only later did it become known by the name *Pterodactylus antiquus* — "old flight-finger" — to mark its place as the very first pterosaur to be discovered.

Not everyone was convinced, however, that a completely new life-form had been unearthed. Friedrich Blumenbach, for example, a Professor of Medicine and an expert on anatomy, argued that it was probably a species of waterfowl. This deduction was similar to Collini's in that he thought the creature lived in water. Samuel von Soemmerring, who took over Karl Theodor's collection when it was moved to Munich, went even further. He claimed it was a type of bat, and a link in the evolution between mammals and birds. He even renamed the fossil *Ornithocephalus antiquus* — meaning "old bird-head."

Convincing proof

Not to be discouraged, Cuvier battled on. He studied the creature's fossilized teeth, which showed that they were small; pointed; all the same size, like a reptile's; and different from the variety of shapes found in mammals. He eventually concluded that it was a reptile, one that could fly by flapping a pair of membranes attached to each forearm and an extremely elongated finger. This reptile must have lived on insects and small creatures, which it caught in its slim, tooth-lined beak. It would have been able to totter on its back legs only if it propped itself up on its folded wings. Cuvier's interpretation is still recognized today, and it has helped with the identification of many pterosaur discoveries throughout the world.

PTERODACTYLUS FIND

The skeleton below belongs to the pterosaur **Pterodactylus**, first examined in the eighteenth century by Cosimo Collini, keeper of the Mannheim Natural History Collection, in Germany. Collini, however, did not identify it accurately as the skeleton of a flying reptile.

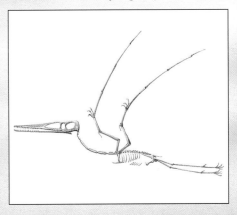

ALONGSIDE THE DINOSAURS

Pterosaurs existed for almost as long as the dinosaurs. They, too, had to adapt to changing conditions and spent most of their time trying to survive. Occasionally, they may even have come to the rescue of certain dinosaur species.

An unearthly screeching pierced the calm of the warm Jurassic day. In the distance, a small group of herbivores looked up from the lush foliage they were devouring. They could hear a group of pterosaurs circling and diving noisily. A huge, hungry carnivore had emerged from the forest to secure its next meal. Fortunately, though, the pterosaurs' timely warning gave the frightened herbivores just enough time to make a run for it.

There is no evidence, of course, that pterosaurs worked together with plant-eating dinosaurs in a common fight for survival against the meat-eaters. But, since herbivores constantly had to be on their guard, and the flying reptiles could screech so effectively, the result may well have been a useful early-warning system.

Small snacks

It seems unlikely, however, that the increasingly large carnivores had much interest in catching pterosaurs. Many of the flying reptiles would have been too small to make an entire meal, since their wingspans reached just about 2 feet (0.6 meter), and they were mostly skin and bone, with little flesh. It would have been much easier to pounce on a slow-moving herbivore than to catch a darting high-flyer.

Some pterosaur fossils that have been found in Italy, however, have their bones tightly packed together. This has led some experts to conclude that the creatures could have provided a tasty snack for a passing dinosaur, which then brought up, or regurgitated, the undigested bones.

Some smaller predators, meanwhile, would have been fast enough to surprise a grounded pterosaur, and may even have been able to pluck flying creatures out of the sky using their strong jaws.

Would a hungry pterosaur ever have been tempted to prey on a dinosaur? Fossils discovered so far indicate that the flying reptiles ate fish and insects as their main diet. In spite of this, some experts claim that huge Late Cretaceous **Quetzalcoatlus**, found in southwestern North America, may have eaten dinosaur remains.

Pterosaurs died out with the last of the dinosaurs at the end of the Cretaceous period, about 65 million years ago. Over the millions of years of their existence, however, new species were evolving and old species were becoming extinct all the time.

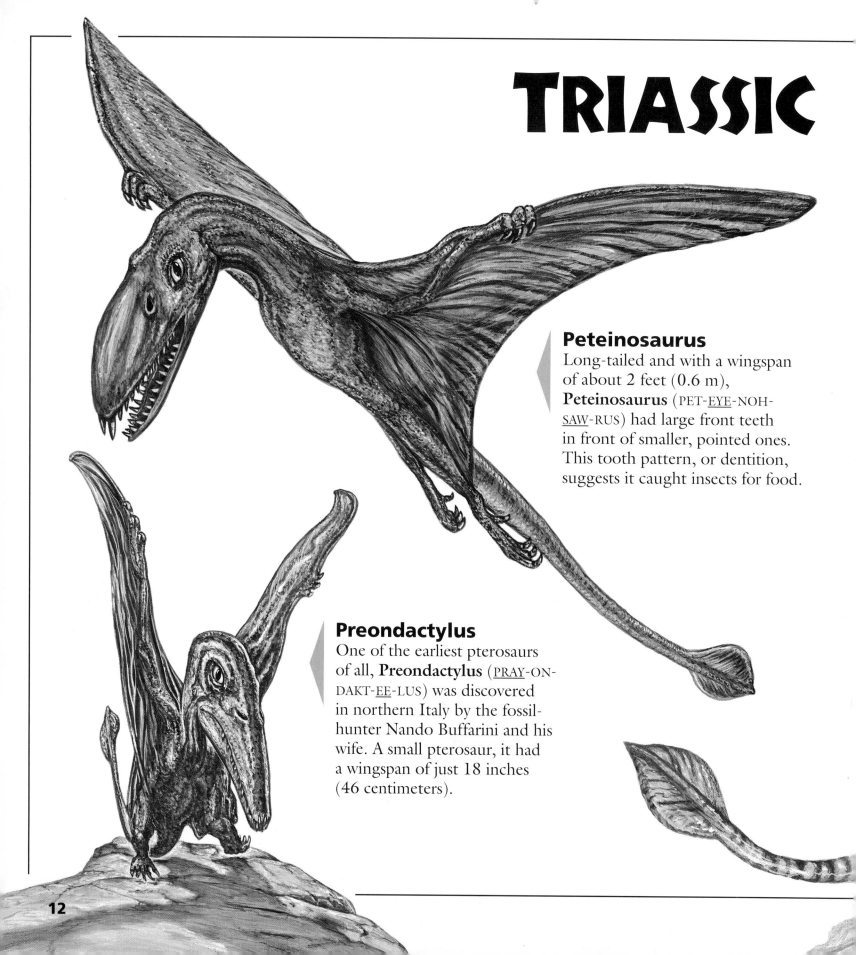

TRIASSIC

Peteinosaurus

Long-tailed and with a wingspan of about 2 feet (0.6 m), **Peteinosaurus** (PET-EYE-NOH-SAW-RUS) had large front teeth in front of smaller, pointed ones. This tooth pattern, or dentition, suggests it caught insects for food.

Preondactylus

One of the earliest pterosaurs of all, **Preondactylus** (PRAY-ON-DAKT-EE-LUS) was discovered in northern Italy by the fossil-hunter Nando Buffarini and his wife. A small pterosaur, it had a wingspan of just 18 inches (46 centimeters).

PTEROSAURS

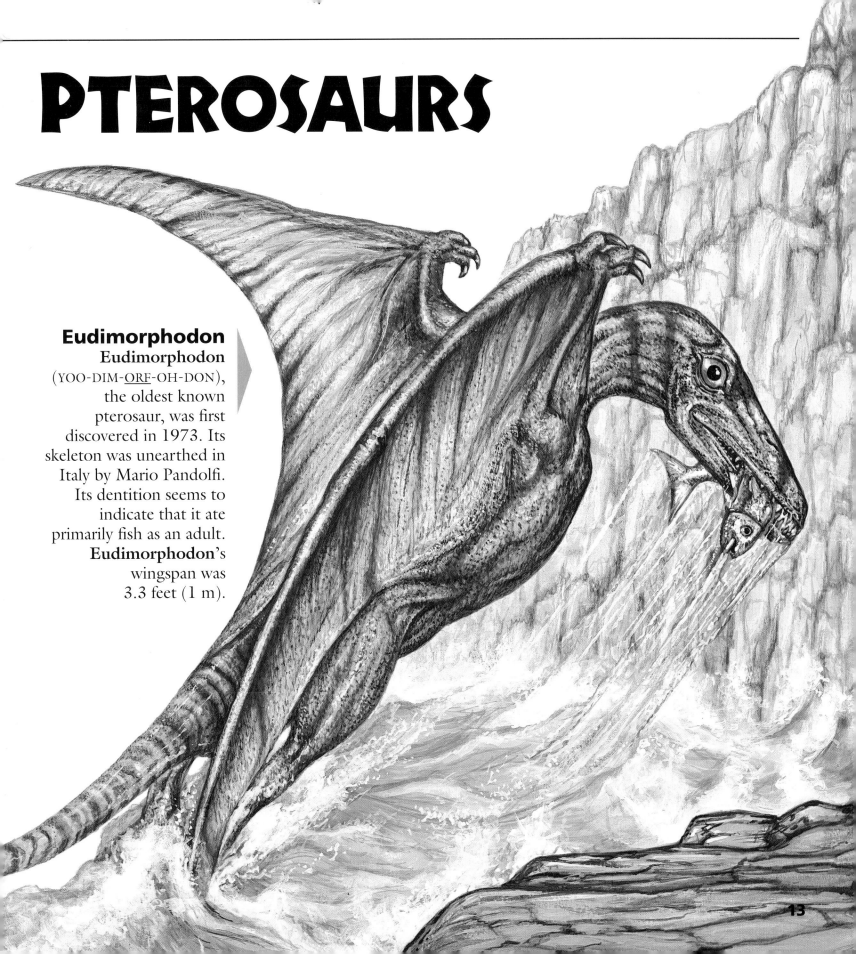

Eudimorphodon
Eudimorphodon
(YOO-DIM-<u>ORF</u>-OH-DON),
the oldest known
pterosaur, was first
discovered in 1973. Its
skeleton was unearthed in
Italy by Mario Pandolfi.
Its dentition seems to
indicate that it ate
primarily fish as an adult.
Eudimorphodon's
wingspan was
3.3 feet (1 m).

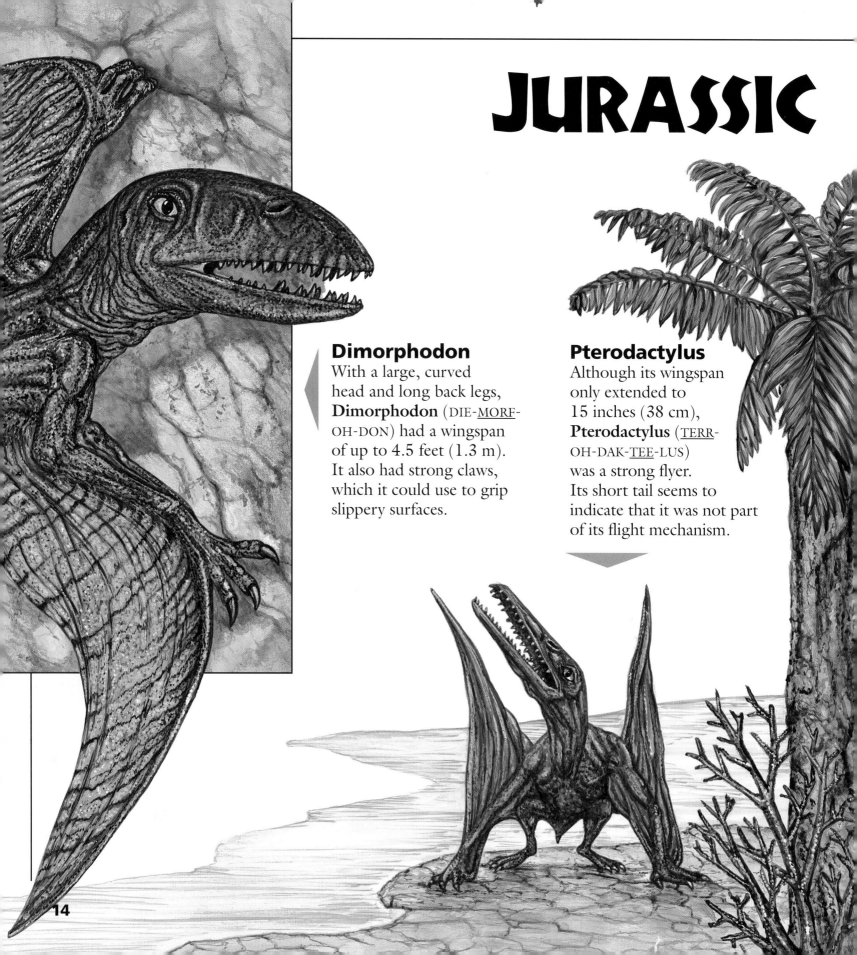

JURASSIC

Dimorphodon
With a large, curved head and long back legs, **Dimorphodon** (DIE-<u>MORF</u>-OH-DON) had a wingspan of up to 4.5 feet (1.3 m). It also had strong claws, which it could use to grip slippery surfaces.

Pterodactylus
Although its wingspan only extended to 15 inches (38 cm), **Pterodactylus** (<u>TERR</u>-OH-DAK-<u>TEE</u>-LUS) was a strong flyer. Its short tail seems to indicate that it was not part of its flight mechanism.

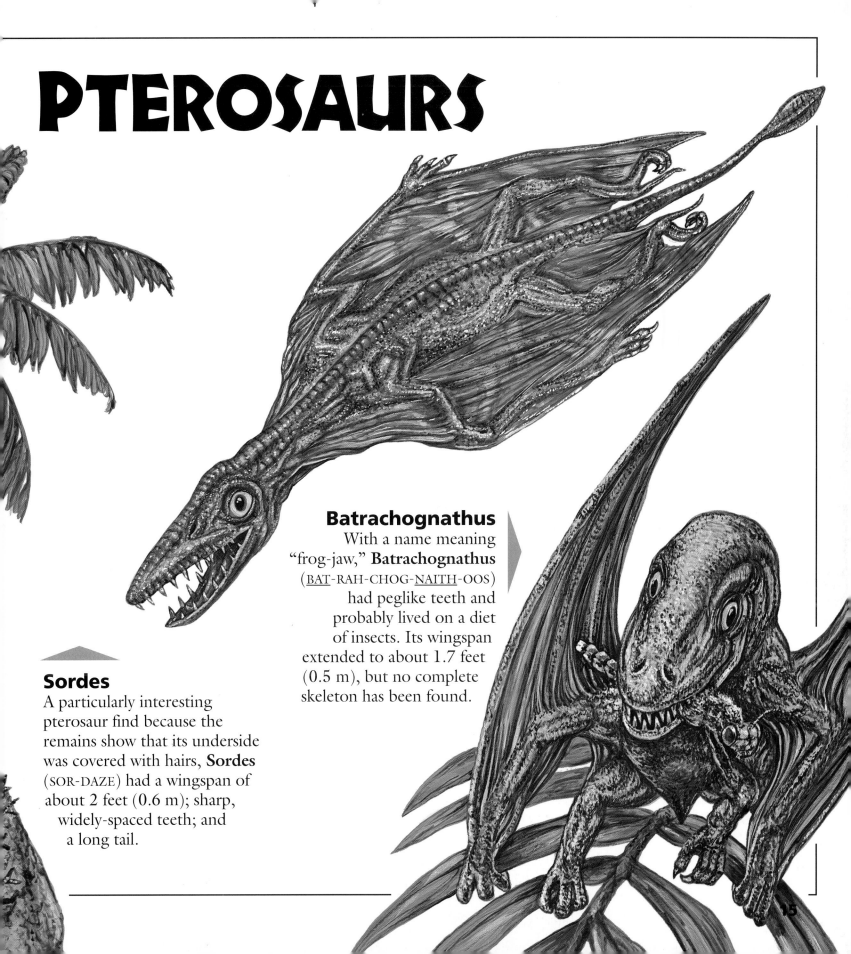

PTEROSAURS

Batrachognathus

With a name meaning "frog-jaw," **Batrachognathus** (<u>BAT</u>-RAH-CHOG-<u>NAITH</u>-OOS) had peglike teeth and probably lived on a diet of insects. Its wingspan extended to about 1.7 feet (0.5 m), but no complete skeleton has been found.

Sordes

A particularly interesting pterosaur find because the remains show that its underside was covered with hairs, **Sordes** (SOR-DAZE) had a wingspan of about 2 feet (0.6 m); sharp, widely-spaced teeth; and a long tail.

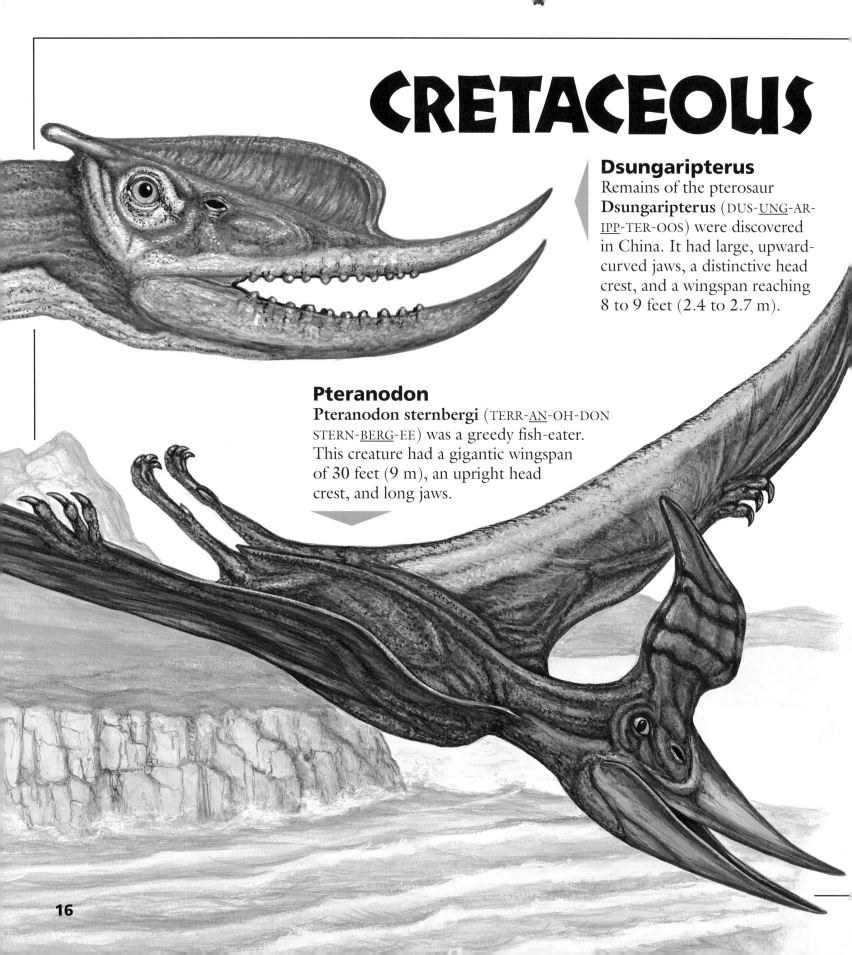

CRETACEOUS

Dsungaripterus

Remains of the pterosaur **Dsungaripterus** (DUS-<u>UNG</u>-AR-<u>IPP</u>-TER-OOS) were discovered in China. It had large, upward-curved jaws, a distinctive head crest, and a wingspan reaching 8 to 9 feet (2.4 to 2.7 m).

Pteranodon

Pteranodon sternbergi (TERR-<u>AN</u>-OH-DON STERN-<u>BERG</u>-EE) was a greedy fish-eater. This creature had a gigantic wingspan of 30 feet (9 m), an upright head crest, and long jaws.

PTEROSAURS

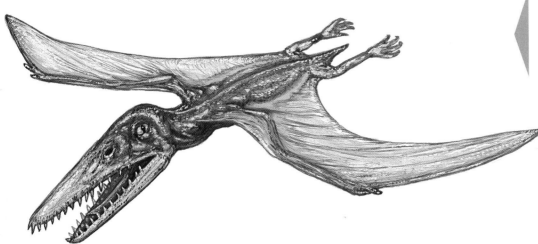

Ornithocheirus
Ornithocheirus (ORN-EETH-OH-CARE-US) was discovered in England. It had strong teeth, a short tail, and a wingspan of over 8 feet (2.4 m). It must have been a prolific species, since many remains have been found.

Pterodaustro
Discovered in Argentina, **Pterodaustro** (TERR-OH-DOW-STROH) had a wingspan of 4.3 feet (1.3 m); very long, upwardly bent jaws; and strange teeth that resembled the bristles of a brush — ideal for sifting out small fish.

17

HOW DID THEY FLY?

Almost everyone knows that birds need their feathers to fly, and airplanes have wings powered by engines to propel them skyward. But if the prehistoric pterosaurs had neither, how did they manage to stay aloft?

For a second, **Ornithodesmus** seemed to pause in mid-flight. The magnificent sweep of its wing bones — its forelimbs — curved gracefully between tapering ends to form a perfect arc. The flight membranes, stretching between these bones and the creature's body, arched gently upward like shallow umbrellas. Then, suddenly, with a single flapping motion, **Ornithodesmus** catapulted forward and downward, ready to snap an unsuspecting fish out of the water on its descent.

Powered flight

Pterosaurs were undoubtedly skilled aviators, but how did they actually launch into flight? Some experts claim that they became fast runners and, when they fluttered the membranes attached to their forelimbs, their speed gave them enough "lift" to enable them to leave the ground. Others, however, believe that these reptiles launched themselves from trees — they had sharply clawed feet that would have been ideal for climbing — and used air currents to soar for short distances before gliding gently to the ground.

All in a flap

Whatever the method of flight, no pterosaur would have stayed in the air for long unless it could flap its membranes; and, from fossils dug up all over the world, scientists have concluded that these creatures could do just that. A pterosaur's jointed forelimbs, which consisted of a short upper armbone, longer forearm bones, a wrist that could be rotated in several angles, and an extremely long fourth finger, were supported by powerful chest muscles. When flexed, these muscles pulled the forelimbs up and down in a flapping motion. Scientists have also found fossil remains at Solnhofen in Germany that show the flight membranes in perfect detail. The membranes' thin film of skin was full of tiny, hornlike fibers. These would flex the membranes to give them an umbrella shape so that there was greater air pressure below the membrane than above it. This way, the pterosaur could soar into the air.

Hollow bones

Why didn't the weight of these creatures bring them back down to Earth with a thud? The answer

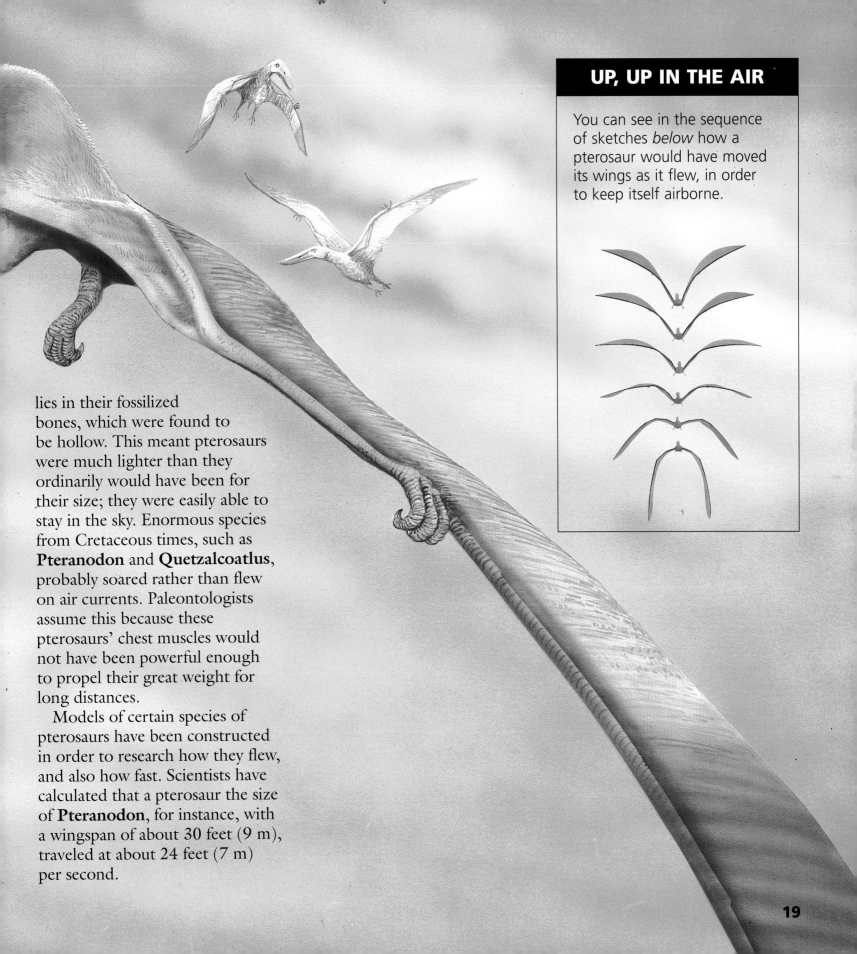

You can see in the sequence of sketches *below* how a pterosaur would have moved its wings as it flew, in order to keep itself airborne.

lies in their fossilized bones, which were found to be hollow. This meant pterosaurs were much lighter than they ordinarily would have been for their size; they were easily able to stay in the sky. Enormous species from Cretaceous times, such as **Pteranodon** and **Quetzalcoatlus**, probably soared rather than flew on air currents. Paleontologists assume this because these pterosaurs' chest muscles would not have been powerful enough to propel their great weight for long distances.

Models of certain species of pterosaurs have been constructed in order to research how they flew, and also how fast. Scientists have calculated that a pterosaur the size of **Pteranodon**, for instance, with a wingspan of about 30 feet (9 m), traveled at about 24 feet (7 m) per second.

HANGING AROUND

Pterosaurs, like birds, did not spend all their time flying. They came down regularly to sleep, feed their young, and rest.

Germanodactylus was tired after a day of soaring over the Jurassic seas, into which it had dived to fish for food. The setting sun was casting a fiery glow over the waters, and it was time to rest.

It was not easy to sleep with such huge wings buckling at uncomfortable angles around its body, but **Germanodactylus** had found the perfect solution. It would use its sharp foot claws to clamp on to a branch and then hang upside down.

Rigid tails

Experts are not completely in agreement, however, as to whether all pterosaurs actually slept upside down like bats. The long-tailed species, for instance, would probably have found it physically impossible to hang from a branch with their short back legs because their rigid, unbendable tails would have been in the way.

Tucked up for the night

Short-tailed species, however, such as **Germanodactylus** and its close cousin **Pterodactylus**, might have found the upside-down position convenient for folding their voluminous wings. One scientist, Othenio Abel from Germany, even suggested that these creatures may have completely enveloped themselves in their wings as they hung from a branch, like giant pods.

Convenient launchpad

Pterosaurs certainly had enough strength in their hind limbs and claws to hold their weight. Being suspended from a tree would have given them a perfect launchpad for flight. With their forearms free, the pterosaurs could simply drop and spread their wings, catching a current of air that would then waft them skyward.

Coming back to Earth did not present a problem, either. The pterosaur would simply glide in a slow descent, touch down with its hind limbs, and fold its wings so that its three hand digits could also touch the ground. A perfect landing!

Resting afloat?

Some scientists have suggested that pterosaurs may have been able to swim or at least were able to rest on the water and float. They believe this is possible because of webs found between the reptiles' toes. Other experts, however, contradict this theory; they believe pterosaur wings were much too wide and bulky to permit this. Whatever the situation, the pterosaurs almost certainly skimmed across the water's surface in search of unsuspecting fish that could be gobbled down.

NESTING HABITS

Pterosaurs were reptiles, and experts believe they probably built nests in which to lay their eggs. But where did they do this, and what happened to pterosaur babies once they had hatched?

The baby **Ornithocheirus** could hardly wait. The minute its mother touched down on the slippery coastal rocks, it plunged its whole head into her opening jaws. Breakfast at last! There, in the food pouch, bulging from her lower jaw, was a shiny, shredded, little fish. The meal was devoured instantly, and the greedy offspring closed its eyes contentedly.

A young pterosaur probably started life as an egg. Fossilized shells found near remains are small enough to have belonged to these flying reptiles, although no one is certain they are pterosaur eggs. Experts agree that if pterosaurs did lay eggs, their eggs must have been very small, so the hatchlings would have been small at birth, too. So far, no one has found the remains of a pterosaur with an egg inside its body; nor do experts know for sure whether the remains that they have found belonged to males or females.

Making a nest

Such small hatchlings would not have been able to fly or catch their own food, and they would have had to be looked after by one or both parents for a while. A nest, therefore, would have been essential for a growing pterosaur family. This nest might have been built out of earth scraped together using long-clawed feet, or perhaps fashioned from fallen foliage into a hollow shape.

Caring parents

Here, a pterosaur parent may have sat on its eggs to keep them warm. Or, it may have positioned the nest in the sunlight, in order to allow natural warmth to incubate its offspring. Once safely hatched, experts believe the helpless baby pterosaurs would have been guarded by one parent while the other foraged for food, just as many birds do today.

Some species may even have congregated in hatching colonies, leaving all the eggs in the care of one or two adults. The food-hunters would scoop up prey — either fish or insects — and bring back this food in their jaws, possibly half-digested so that the baby reptiles could eat easily. Pterosaurs were almost certainly intelligent enough to be caring, attentive parents.

FEEDING TIME

The type of teeth a pterosaur had gives experts a clue as to what it ate. Some fossil finds have even yielded perfectly preserved stomach contents!

With a flick of its tail membrane, which acted as a rudder, **Rhamphorhynchus** steered itself earthward. The shimmering fish gliding just below the surface of the sea had only seconds to live. Powerful jaws now seized its body, and razor-sharp teeth bore into its flesh as it was hauled out of the water and swept aloft. The pterosaur could look forward to a tasty meal. **Pterodactylus**, meanwhile, far below on the rocks, was already eating an earlier catch.

A half-eaten, primitive **Leptolepides** fish, discovered with the bones of a small **Rhamphorhynchus** at Solnhofen, Germany, proves that some pterosaurs were fish-eaters. This pterosaur had rows of sharp teeth along its upper and lower jaws, which were long and slender.

It would zoom close to the sea's surface and trawl its lower jaw in the water, clamping down hard with the upper jaw on any fish that it met. A small pouch of skin on the lower jaw may have been used to store the fish, perhaps in a first stage of digestion. At times, however, the pterosaur may have saved prey to feed to its young, once it returned to its nest.

Different teeth

Without such a fearsome array of teeth, however, other pterosaurs had to satisfy themselves with smaller prey. Species such as Jurassic **Gnathosaurus** and **Ctenochasma**, for example, had jaws lined with large numbers of thin, fine teeth that were unsuited to biting. Instead, these reptiles used the teeth for filtering out small marine creatures from the

mouthfuls of water that they scooped up while standing in the shallows. **Pterodaustro**, meanwhile, had short, blunt teeth set into its upper jaw. These were ideal for mashing its food into even tinier pieces.

Flying food

Other pterosaurs may have lived on a diet of insects, which they caught on the wing. Pterosaur species such as Late Jurassic **Anurognathus**, for example, had smaller heads and wider mouths than their fish-eating companions — ideal for gobbling down tasty dragonflies!

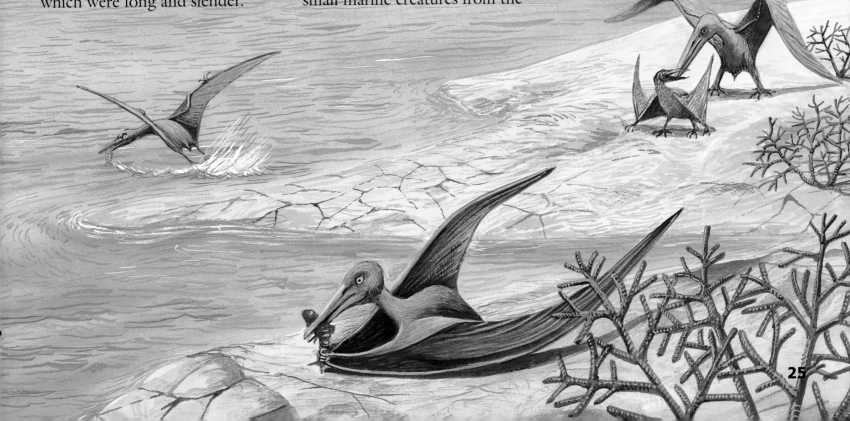

THE BIGGEST PTEROSAUR OF ALL

Over millions of years, pterosaurs developed and grew from small-winged creatures until, in Late Cretaceous times, monsters the size of today's light aircraft darkened the skies.

Soaring creatures cast dark shadows on the prehistoric land as a passing herd of dinosaurs scanned the skies for the source of all this thunderous, overhead flapping. A group of mighty **Quetzalcoatlus** had taken to the air again.

Neither before nor since have there been such enormous flying creatures. Fossilized remains found in Big Bend National Park in Texas by Douglas Lawson in 1971 show that **Quetzalcoatlus** lived right at the end of Cretaceous times. What a magnificent creature it must have been! Judging from the fossils of a single wing that Lawson discovered (other bones and skeletons have been unearthed since then), scientists can tell that **Quetzalcoatlus** probably had a

wingspan of 39 feet (12 m). It was about the size of a modern-day light aircraft. It weighed much less than these modern machines, however — only 190 pounds (86 kilograms) — about the same as an average adult human male. Without the hollow bones that kept down the weight of its huge frame, **Quetzalcoatlus** would otherwise never have been able to leave the ground.

Giant fish-eater
Without doubt, everything about **Quetzalcoatlus**'s body was giant-sized.

It was named after Quetzalcoatl, the feathered serpent-god of the Aztecs, an ancient people

of Central America. It had a huge, long head with an elongated crest, which topped a long neck so rigid that **Quetzalcoatlus** had difficulty moving it from side to side. Its thin jaws were toothless, and some experts think

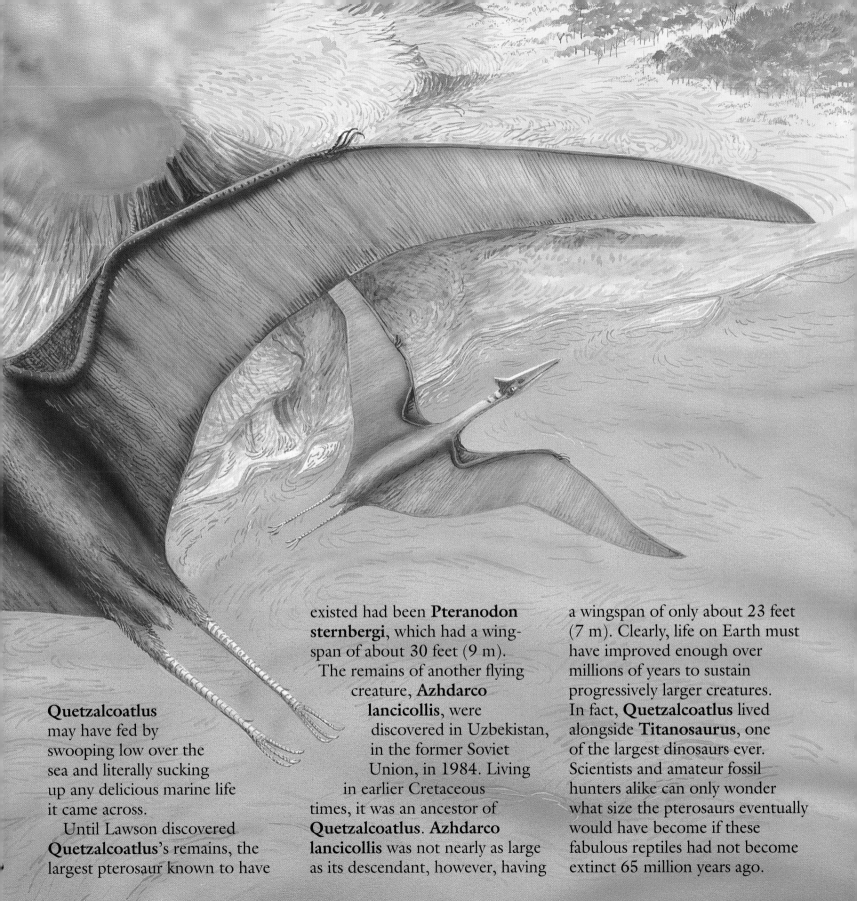

Quetzalcoatlus may have fed by swooping low over the sea and literally sucking up any delicious marine life it came across.

Until Lawson discovered **Quetzalcoatlus**'s remains, the largest pterosaur known to have existed had been **Pteranodon sternbergi**, which had a wingspan of about 30 feet (9 m).

The remains of another flying creature, **Azhdarco lancicollis**, were discovered in Uzbekistan, in the former Soviet Union, in 1984. Living in earlier Cretaceous times, it was an ancestor of **Quetzalcoatlus**. **Azhdarco lancicollis** was not nearly as large as its descendant, however, having a wingspan of only about 23 feet (7 m). Clearly, life on Earth must have improved enough over millions of years to sustain progressively larger creatures. In fact, **Quetzalcoatlus** lived alongside **Titanosaurus**, one of the largest dinosaurs ever. Scientists and amateur fossil hunters alike can only wonder what size the pterosaurs eventually would have become if these fabulous reptiles had not become extinct 65 million years ago.

SHARING THE PREHISTORIC SKIES

Several other types of prehistoric creatures also propelled themselves through the air by various means — including one that many scientists believe may have been among the first true birds.

As a gentle evening breeze stirred the foliage at the edge of a prehistoric forest, **Daedalosaurus**, *opposite top*, spread its wing flaps and took advantage of the light air currents to glide noiselessly out of high branches down to the ground. Tiny **Longisquama**, *opposite bottom*, also felt confident enough to flex the scaly spines that grew from its back and jumped the short distance to a smooth rock. **Draco**, *below left*, meanwhile, had already descended to balance on a low-lying fern.

But most magnificent of this group was undoubtedly **Archaeopteryx**, *above left*. It had feathered wings that enabled it to soar effortlessly from the ground into the prehistoric trees.

Many small flying creatures from the time of the dinosaurs, such as the ones shown on these two pages, relied on flaps of skin attached to their bodies between their front and back limbs to lift them off the ground. They were able to glide through the air, rather than fly.

Draco could glide the farthest. It could travel up to 200 feet (60 m) in one bound, even though it had the smallest flaps of any prehistoric flying creature discovered so far, measuring only 4 inches (10 cm) from edge to edge. These flaps served **Draco** well, however, because it has survived to this day. It lives in the jungles of Southeast Asia and is known as the **Flying Dragon**.

Folding flaps

Daedalosaurus — named after the ancient Greek hero Daedalus, who built himself wings in order to escape from captivity — was a sturdier creature. It was lizardlike in appearance with four limbs and a long, stiff tail. This gliding reptile, when fully grown, could have had an overall length of 16-18 inches (40-45 cm) and could maneuver itself through the air by expanding its flexible rib cage and spreading out its flaps. Once at its destination, it would then fold up the flaps close to its body to prevent them from catching on thick foliage.

Taking off

Longisquama had a unique method of getting around. Along its back were two rows of overlapping, scaly shafts that usually lay flat. When it wanted to take to the air, however, it would raise these structures to form large, flat surfaces that would lift **Longisquama** gracefully over short distances.

Early birds

Archaeopteryx was distinctive in that its fossilized remains show it was covered in feathers. From the skeletons discovered so far, we also know that it had an elongated skull with tooth-lined jaws, long forelimbs with flappable membranes attached, and a lengthy, rigid tail. Some of these last characteristics made it seem reptilian.

Thought to have been a form of early bird dating from late Jurassic times, **Archaeopteryx** probably fluttered around, but it would have been a poor aviator in comparison with the pterosaurs. Its wings were not as developed as those in modern birds. Somehow, however, early birds managed to survive after the pterosaurs became extinct 65 million years ago, evolving to become the birds that populate our world today.

GLOSSARY

anatomy — the arrangement and relationship of the parts of a living thing.

array — an orderly grouping or arrangement of materials.

aviators — animals or people that fly.

carnivorous — relating to a meat-eating animal.

catapulted — thrown or launched into the air.

colonies — groups of animals or other organisms that live together.

congregated — gathered or collected into a group or crowd.

Cretaceous times — the final era of the dinosaurs, lasting from 144-65 million years ago.

dentition — the number and arrangement of teeth within an animal's mouth.

devour — to eat up quickly or in a greedy way.

elongated — drawn out; made longer.

evolution — the process in which an organism adapts, or changes, over a period of time to suit changing environments or conditions.

foliage — the leaves of a tree, shrub, or plant.

forage — to wander or roam in search of food; to graze or browse.

forelimbs — the front arms, legs, fins, or wings of an animal.

fossilized — embedded and preserved in rocks, resin, or other material.

gaping — opened widely, like a yawning mouth.

hatchlings — baby animals, such as birds or some reptiles, that have recently broken out of their eggs, or hatched.

herbivorous — plant-eating.

instinctively — behaving in a way that is natural, or automatic, rather than learned.

Jurassic times — the middle era of the dinosaurs, lasting from 213-144 million years ago.

marine — of or relating to the sea or ocean.

membrane — a thin, flexible layer of tissue in or on the body of an animal or plant.

paleontologists — scientists who study geologic periods of the past as they are known from fossil remains.

preserved — protected; maintained or kept from decay.

primitive — in an early stage of development; not highly developed or evolved.

prolific — producing young or fruit in great numbers; very productive.

propel — to cause or drive something to move forward.

pterosaurs — members of a group of extinct flying reptiles.

remains — something left over; a dead body.

reptile — cold-blooded, mostly egg-laying animals, such as lizards, turtles, and many prehistoric creatures.

rudder — the movable piece at the rear of a boat or airplane that is used for steering.

staple — something used or needed regularly; a main feature or part.

Triassic times — the first era of the dinosaurs, lasting from 249-213 millions years ago.

unearthed — dug out of the ground; discovered.

voluminous — very large; bulky.

MORE BOOKS TO READ

Archaeopteryx: The First Bird. Elizabeth J. Sandell (Bancroft-Sage)

Dinosaurs: Monster Reptiles of a Bygone Era. Secrets of the Animal World (series). Eulalia García (Gareth Stevens)

Dinosaurs of the Land, Sea, and Air. Michael Teitelbaum (Rourke Enterprises)

Draw, Model, and Paint (series): *Dinosaurs* (3 of 6 vols.). Isidro Sanchez (Gareth Stevens)

Flyers. Prehistoric Zoobooks. J. Wexo (Creative Educ.)

Flying Dragons: Ancient Reptiles That Ruled the Air. David Eldridge (Troll Associates)

The New Dinosaur Collection (series). (Gareth Stevens)

Pterosaurs, the Flying Reptiles. Helen Roney Sattler (Lothrop, Lee & Shepard Books)

The Search for the Origin of Birds. Lawrence Witmer (Franklin Watts)

World of Dinosaurs (series). (Gareth Stevens)

VIDEOS

Dinosaurs. (DeBeck Educational Video)

Dinosaurs! (Golden Book Video)

Dinosaurs and Other Prehistoric Animals. (Seesaw Video)

Dinosaurs and Strange Creatures. (Concord Video)

Dinosaurs, Dinosaurs, Dinosaurs. (Twin Tower Enterprises)

Nova: The Case of the Flying Dinosaur. (Live Home Video)

WEB SITES

home.stlnet.com/~azero/Pterosaur_Homepage.htm

www.dinodon.com/index.html

www.dinosauria.com/

www.dinosociety.org/

www.fmnh./org/exhibits/previous/arch/press.htm

www.ZoomDinosaurs.com

Due to the dynamic nature of the Internet, some web sites stay current longer than others. To find additional web sites, use a reliable search engine with one or more of the following keywords to help you locate more information about dinosaurs. Keywords: *archaeopteryx, dinosaurs, fossils, paleontology, pteranodon, pterosaurs.*

INDEX